A Paines Plough and Theatr Clwyd production

Dexter and Winter's Detective Agency

by Nathan Bryon

Supported using public funding by
ARTS COUNCIL
ENGLAND

Cyngor Celfyddydau Cymru
Arts Council of Wales

Dexter and Winter's Detective Agency

by Nathan Bryon

Cast

ANGELA/CARRIE/KID 1, 2, 3/ GRANNY ANNIE/CALLUM CHARITY BUCKET/BOSSMAN/BARLADY/ BILL THE BUTCHER/KATHY COSTUME LADY/JEFF / ZEBRA MAN/TICKET INSPECTOR/POLICE OFFICER	Charlotte Bate
WINTER	Charlotte O'Leary
DEXTER	Toyin Omari-Kinch

Production Team

Direction	Stef O'Driscoll
Lighting	Peter Small
Sound & Original Music	Dominic Kennedy
Movement	Annie-Lunnette Deakin-Foster
Movement Associate	Hayley Chilvers
Assistant Director	Janisè Sadik
Lighting Programmer	Tom Davis
Producer for Paines Plough	Sofia Stephanou
Producer for Theatr Clwyd	Nick Stevenson
Company Stage Manager	Rachel Graham
Technical Stage Manager	Wesley Hughes
Costume Supervisor	Alison Hartnell

NATHAN BRYON (Writer)

Nathan Bryon is a writer and actor, who grew up eating as much Uxbridge Road Caribbean food as his bank balance would allow. He is best known to viewers for his role as regular character Jamie in SOME GIRLS and BENIDORM's sunniest holiday maker, Joey Ellis.

Nathan has written for critically acclaimed CBeebies' animation RASTAMOUSE, BAFTA award-winning SWASHBUCKLE and on all three series of BAFTA nominated APPLE TREE HOUSE (CBeebies) alongside BAFTA winning GIGGLEBIZ.

In 2017 Nathan's one-man show MIXED BRAIN, a show about his mixed heritage, premiered in ROUNDABOUT at the Edinburgh Festival Fringe.

Nathan has secured a three-picture book deal with Penguin Random House. His first book LOOK UP! will hit shelves in the US and UK in June 2019.

In addition, Nathan has recently co-written a Sky Arts short NEW BLOOD starring Samson Kayo and Jane Horrocks; this can be found to watch on NOW TV and Sky On Demand. NEW BLOOD is currently being developed by Sky One.

One of Nathan's passions is creating his own work about his black British experience. He created REALITY, a comedic social commentary ethnology series, which has had two solo premiers at the BFI in NFT1. REALITY has also screened and won various awards around the world at film festivals. Nathan is currently writing series 3.0.

Nathan has various TV projects in development with Roughcut, Three Stones Media, and a feature film in development with Damian Jones and Adam Rolston.

CHARLOTTE BATE (Angela/ Carrie/Kid 1, 2, 3/Granny Annie/ Callum Charity Bucket/Bossman/ Barlady/Bill The Butcher/Kathy Costume Lady/Jeff / Zebra Man/ Ticket Inspector/Police Officer)

Charlotte trained at The Guildhall School of Music and Drama.

Theatre credits include: BLACKTHORN (West Yorkshire Playhouse/Edinburgh Festival); THE RIVALS (Watermill Theatre); KING LEAR (Orange Tree Theatre); WATERSHIP DOWN (Watermill Theatre); ROMEO AND JULIET (Sheffield Crucible).

Television credits include: CASUALTY (BBC); THE WHITE HOUSE FARM MURDERS (ITV) and PHILIP K. DICK'S ELECTRIC DREAMS (Channel 4).

Radio credits include: DOCTOR WHO THE PRIMEVAL DESIGN.

CHARLOTTE O'LEARY (Winter)

Charlotte trained at the Royal Welsh College of Music and Drama.

Theatre credits include: ROUNDABOUT 2018 Season directed by Stef O'Driscoll: ISLAND TOWN, STICKS AND STONES, HOW TO SPOT AN ALIEN (Paines Plough/Theatr Clwyd); UNDER MILK WOOD directed by Brendan O'Hea (Watermill Theatre); HUSH directed by Hannah Bannister (Paines Plough/RWCMD).

Television credits include: THE WITCHER (Netflix Originals).

Radio credits include: TORCHWOOD directed by Scott Handcock (Big Finish Productions).

TOYIN OMARI-KINCH (Dexter)

Toyin Omari-Kinch is an established actor who recently played David Taylor for over a year in WAR HORSE at the National Theatre and during a national tour of the production. He and the production received fantastic reviews.

Toyin played the role of Eric the Archer in the RSC and National Theatre of Scotland's US tour of DUNSINANE. The show was adapted by David Greig and directed by Roxana Silbert and went to North Carolina, Washington, Chicago and Los Angeles. He has also appeared in numerous productions for the Birmingham Rep.

On the small screen, he has featured in DOCTORS for the BBC.

STEF O'DRISCOLL (Direction)
Stef is Artistic Director of nabokov and previously Associate Director at Paines Plough and Lyric Hammersmith.

As director, theatre includes: ISLAND TOWN, STICKS AND STONES, HOW TO SPOT AN ALIEN (Paines Plough/Theatr Clwyd); WITH A LITTLE BIT OF LUCK, HOPELESSLY DEVOTED (Paines Plough/Birmingham REP/Latitude); BLISTER (Paines Plough/RWCMD); LAST NIGHT (nabokov/Roundhouse); STORYTELLING ARMY (nabokov/Brighton Festival); SLUG (nabokov/Latitude); BOX CLEVER (nabokov); YARD GAL (Ovalhouse); THE UNMASTER, A TALE FROM THE BEDSIT (Roundhouse/Bestival); FINDING HOME (Roundhouse); A GUIDE TO SECOND DATE SEX, WHEN WOMEN WEE (Underbelly/Soho Theatre); A MIDSUMMER NIGHT'S DREAM [co-director] (Lyric Hammersmith).

As Associate Director, theatre includes: MOGADISHU (Lyric Hammersmith/Royal Exchange Theatre, Manchester).

As Assistant Director, theatre includes: WASTED (Paines Plough); HENRY IV (Donmar Warehouse/St Anne's Warehouse, Brooklyn); BLASTED (Lyric Hammersmith).

Upcoming projects include: A HISTORY OF WATER IN THE MIDDLE EAST (Royal Court Theatre); LIT (Nottingham Playhouse/HighTide).

Awards include: WITH A LITTLE BIT OF LUCK (BBC Radio & Music Award for Best Production); YARD GAL (Fringe Report Award for Best Fringe Production).

PETER SMALL (Lighting)
Peter is an Offie and Theatre & Technology Award-nominated lighting designer working across theatre, dance and opera. He regularly collaborates with Paines Plough, including lighting productions in their pop-up theatre ROUNDABOUT.

Recent lighting design for theatre includes: RADIO (Arcola Theatre); SQUARE GO (59E59 New York, Francesca Moody Productions); AD LIBIDO (Soho Theatre); YOU STUPID DARKNESS! (Paines Plough/Theatre Royal Plymouth); ROUNDABOUT 2018 Season: HOW TO SPOT AN ALIEN, STICKS AND STONES and ISLAND TOWN (Paines Plough/Theatr Clwyd); SQUARE GO (Francesca Moody Productions); ROUNDABOUT 2017 Season: OUT OF LOVE, BLACK MOUNTAIN (Offie-nominated) and HOW TO BE A KID (Paines Plough/Theatr Clwyd/Orange Tree Theatre); PLASTIC (Poleroid Theatre/Old Red Lion); OLD FOOLS (Southwark Playhouse); Offie and Theatre & Technology Award-nominated A GIRL IN SCHOOL UNIFORM (WALKS INTO A BAR) (New Diorama); FOX (Old Red Lion); MEMORY OF LEAVES (UK tour); SHE CALLED ME MOTHER (Pitch Lake Productions/UK tour); THE VENUS FACTOR (MTA Academy/Bridewell Theatre); EAST END BOYS AND WEST END GIRLS (Arcola Theatre/tour); A MIDSUMMER NIGHT'S DREAM, FREE ASSOCIATION and CRAZY LADY (Forum Alpbach, Austria); RICHARD III and BARD ON BOARD 2 (Royal Court/Queen Mary 2 Ocean Liner).

Opera and musical theatre include: THE RAPE OF LUCRETIA (Stratford Circus); ALL OR NOTHING (West End/tour); CINDERELLA (Loughborough Theatre); TOM & JERRY (EventBox Theatre, Egypt). Peter was revival lighting designer on KISS ME KATE for Oper Graz.

Upcoming projects include BABY REINDEER, DO OUR BEST at Edinburgh Festival Fringe; SPIDERFLY (Theatre503); LIT (Nottingham Playhouse/HighTide) and taking AD LIBIDO and SQUARE GO on tour.

DOMINIC KENNEDY (Sound & Original Music)

Dominic Kennedy is a sound designer and music producer for performance and live events; he has a keen interest in developing new work and implementing sound and music at an early stage in a creative process. Dominic is a graduate from Royal Central School of Speech and Drama, where he developed specialist skills in collaborative and devised theatre making, music composition and installation practices. His work often fuses found sound, field recordings, music composition and synthesis.

Recent design credits include: 17 (WILDCARD); YOU STUPID DARKNESS! (Paines Plough/Theatre Royal Plymouth); POP MUSIC (Paines Plough/Birmingham REP/Latitude); SKATE HARD TURN LEFT (Battersea Arts Centre); ROUNDABOUT 2018 SEASON (Paines Plough/Theatr Clwyd); ANGRY ALAN (Soho Theatre); THE ASSASSINATION OF KATIE HOPKINS (Theatr Clwyd); WITH A LITTLE BIT OF LUCK (Paines Plough/BBC Radio 1Xtra); RAMONA TELLS JIM (Bush Theatre); AND THE REST OF ME FLOATS (Outbox); I AM A TREE (Jamie Wood); BOX CLEVER (nabokov).

ANNIE-LUNNETTE DEAKIN-FOSTER (Movement)

Annie-Lunnette Deakin-Foster is a passionate contemporary dance theatre choreographer, maker and movement director and is a co-founding member of award-winning company, C-12 Dance Theatre.

Recent theatre credits include: YOU STUPID DARKNESS! by Sam Steiner, directed by James Grieve (Paines Plough/Theatre Royal Plymouth); GRIMM TALES, Phillip Pullman's collection adapted by Philip Wilson, directed by Kirsty Housley (Unicorn Theatre); JERICHO'S ROSE by Althea Theatre (Hope & Anchor); POP MUSIC by Anna Jordan, directed by James Grieve (Birmingham REP/Barry Jackson tour/Paines Plough national tour); THE COURT MUST HAVE A QUEEN by Ade Solanke, directed by Sam Curtis Lindsay (Hampton Court Palace); THESE BRIDGES by Phoebe Eclair-Powell (WCYT as part of National Theatre Connections at the Bush); THE LITTLE MATCH GIRL AND OTHER HAPPIER TALES by Joel Horwood and Emma Rice (Shakespeare's Globe/Bristol Old Vic/national tour); THE DARK ROOM by Angela Betzien (Theatre503); I KNOW ALL THE SECRETS OF MY WORLD by Natalie Ibu (tiata fahodzi/national tour).

Recent dance credits include: FORCE (Abbey Road Studios/Imagine Festival Watford/Greenwich & Docklands International Festival/Netherlands); SHHH! (Dance City/MAC Birmingham/Norwich Playhouse/The Woodville Gravesend/CircoMedia Bristol/Winchester Theatre Royal); THE VAN MAN (Watch This Space at the National/St Albans Festival/Freedom Festival Hull/The Albany Outdoors).

JANISÈ SADIK (Assistant Director)
Janisè Sadik is an emerging
theatremaker and director. She is
Paines Plough's Trainee Director for
2019 and was a part of the Young
Vic Directors program and
completed her Boris Karloff
Foundation in 2017. She has been a
co-workshop leader at Park Theatre
leading the Creative Learning
Programme since 2015 directing the
end of term showcase. She's
facilitated in various creative
buildings such as Hoxton Hall, Lyric
Hammersmith, Ovalhouse and
Wimbledon College of Arts. In 2018
she set up a Youth Theatre company
at We Are Spotlight working with
young actors that don't have access
to training. She has worked
internationally in rural parts of
South India to run creative theatre
projects with young children to
empower and build their
confidence. She enjoys work that is
experimental, devised and brings
new writing to life.

Theatre credits as director include:
MILK & OREOS, winner of the
Pandora Award 2015, co-written by
Janisè Sadik & Seraphina Beh
(Melanin Box Festival); BREAKING
THE INTERNET (Ovalhouse Summer
School 2017); BLURRED LINES
(Etcetera Theatre); US by Priscilla
Lafayette Kwabi (Camden People's
Theatre); HYDRAULIC by Tristan
Fynn-Aiduenu (Wimbledon College
of Arts).

Film credits as director include: SHE
by Andrè James.

**RACHEL GRAHAM (Company
Stage Manager)**
Rachel is a freelance stage manager
based in London. She graduated in
2016 with a 1st Class BA (Hons)
Stage Management from Rose
Bruford College of Theatre and
Performance.

Theatre credits include: RAGS (Hope
Mill Theatre/Aria Entertainment);
CRAZY FOR YOU (Mountview at
Pleasance); ROBIN HOOD (Qdos
Productions); THE POLITICAL
HISTORY Of SMACK AND CRACK
(Edinburgh/Soho Theatre/W14
Productions); BLACKTHORN (InSite,
Roundabout @ Edinburgh); LONELY
PLANET (Trafalgar Studios); NOT
TALKING (defibrillator/Arcola
Theatre); A NIGHT AT THE OSCARS
(Aria Entertainment); ALADDIN
(Qdos Productions); WHITE
CHRISTMAS (Curtain Call
Productions/Crewe Lyceum); 31
HOURS (W14 Productions/Bunker
Theatre); SOME LOVERS (Aria
Entertainment/The Other Palace);
JAM (W14 Productions/Finborough
Theatre); POSH (Can't Think Theatre
Company/Pleasance Theatre); THE
PAJAMA GAME (Urdang Academy at
Pleasance Theatre); CINDERELLA
(First Family Entertainment);
SWEENEY TODD (Royal Academy of
Music/Theatre Royal Stratford East);
SISTER ACT (Curtain Call
Productions/Crewe Lyceum).

PAINES PLOUGH

Paines Plough tours the best new theatre to all four corners of the UK and around the world. Whether you're in Liverpool or Lyme Regis, Brighton or Berwick-Upon-Tweed, a Paines Plough show is coming to a theatre near you soon.

'The lifeblood of the UK's theatre ecosystem' *Guardian*

Paines Plough was formed in 1974 over a pint of Paines Bitter in the Plough pub. Since then we've produced more than 150 new productions by world renowned playwrights like Stephen Jeffreys, Abi Morgan, Sarah Kane, Mark Ravenhill, Dennis Kelly, Mike Bartlett, Kate Tempest and Vinay Patel. We've toured those plays to hundreds of places from Bristol to Belfast to Brisbane.

'That noble company Paines Plough, de facto national theatre of new writing' *Daily Telegraph*

In the past three years we've produced 30 shows and performed them in over 200 places across four continents. We tour to more than 30,000 people a year from Cornwall to the Orkney Islands; in village halls and Off-Broadway, at music festivals and student unions, online and on radio, and in our own pop-up theatre ROUNDABOUT.

Our Programme 2019 premieres the best new British plays touring the length and breadth of the UK in theatres, clubs and pubs everywhere from city centres to seaside towns. ROUNDABOUT hosts a jam-packed Edinburgh Festival Fringe programme and brings mini-festivals to each stop on its nationwide tour. Our COME TO WHERE I'M FROM app features 180 short audio plays available to download free from the App Store and GooglePlay.

'I think some theatre just saved my life' @kate_clement on Twitter

PAINES PLOUGH ● **ROUNDABOUT**

'A beautifully designed masterpiece in engineering.' *The Stage*

ROUNDABOUT is Paines Plough's beautiful portable in-the-round theatre. It's a completely self-contained 168-seat auditorium that flat packs into a single lorry and pops up anywhere from theatres to school halls, sports centres, warehouses, car parks and fields.

We built ROUNDABOUT to tour to places that don't have theatres. ROUNDABOUT travels the length and breadth of the UK bringing the nation's best playwrights and a thrilling theatrical experience to audiences everywhere.

Over the last six years ROUNDABOUT has hosted over 2,000 hours of entertainment for more than 100,000 people in places ranging from a churchyard in Salford to Margate seafront.

ROUNDABOUT was designed by Lucy Osborne and Emma Chapman at Studio Three Sixty in collaboration with Charcoalblue and Howard Eaton.

WINNER of Theatre Building of the Year at The Stage Awards 2014

'ROUNDABOUT wins most beautiful interior venue by far @edfringe.'
@ChaoticKirsty on Twitter

'ROUNDABOUT is a beautiful, magical space. Hidden tech make it Turkish-bath-tranquil but with circus-tent-cheek. Aces.'
@evenicol on Twitter

ROUNDABOUT was made possible thanks to the generous support of the following Trusts and individuals and all who named a seat in ROUNDABOUT.

TRUSTS AND FOUNDATIONS
Andrew Lloyd Webber Foundation
Paul Hamlyn Foundation
Garfield Weston Foundation
J Paul Getty Jnr Charitable Trust
John Ellerman Foundation

CORPORATE
Universal Consolidated Group
Howard Eaton Lighting Ltd
Charcoalblue
Avolites Ltd
Factory Settings
Total Solutions

Pop your name on a seat and help us pop-up around the UK:
www.justgiving.com/fundraising/roundaboutauditorium

www.painesplough.com/roundabout
#ROUNDABOUTPP

Paines Plough

Joint Artistic Directors	James Grieve
	George Perrin
Producer	Sofia Stephanou
Finance and Administration Manager	Svetlana Karadimova
Technical Director	Colin Everitt
Assistant Producer	Christabel Holmes
Marketing and Audience Development Officer	Jo Langdon
Production Assistant	Phillippe Cato
Finance and Administration Assistant	Eman Bhatti
Trainee Producer	Nicky Thirugnanam
Trainee Administrator	Adam Poland
Trainee Director	Janisè Sadik
Production and Marketing Placement	Lacey Ruttley
Admin Placement	Ellie Fitz-Gerald
Press Representative	The Corner Shop PR
Graphic Designer	Michael Windsor-Ungureanu
	Thread Design

Board of Directors

Kim Grant (Chair), Ankur Bahl, Nia Janis, Dennis Kelly, Matthew Littleford, Sarah Mansell, Christopher Millard, Cindy Polemis, Carolyn Saunders and Andrea Stark.

Paines Plough Limited is a company limited by guarantee and a registered charity.
Registered Company no: 1165130
Registered Charity no: 267523

Paines Plough, 2nd Floor, 10 Leake Street, London SE1 7NN
+ 44 (0) 20 7240 4533

office@painesplough.com
www.painesplough.com

 Follow @PainesPlough on Twitter

 Like Paines Plough at facebook.com/PainesPloughHQ

 Follow @painesplough on Instagram

Donate to Paines Plough at justgiving.com/PainesPlough

Theatr
Clwyd

The award-winning Theatr Clwyd is Wales' biggest producing theatre.

Based in Flintshire, the gateway to North Wales, since 1976 Theatr Clwyd has been a cultural powerhouse producing world-class theatre, from the UK Theatre Award-winning musical THE ASSASSINATION OF KATIE HOPKINS and National Theatre and West End Olivier award-winning comedy HOME, I'M DARLING, to the site-specific, immersive THE GREAT GATSBY and its sell-out rock 'n' roll pantomime.

Led by Artistic Director Tamara Harvey and Executive Director Liam Evans-Ford, Theatr Clwyd's world-class team of workshop, wardrobe and scenic artists, props makers and technicians ensure the skills vital to a vibrant theatre industry are nurtured right in the heart of Wales. Alongside the three theatre spaces, cinema, café, bar and art galleries, Theatr Clwyd works with the community in many different guises across all art forms and is recognised as a cultural leader for its cross-generational theatre groups, work in youth justice and diverse programme of arts, health and wellbeing.

Find out more: www.theatrclwyd.com
Tweet us: @ClwydTweets
Follow us: Facebook.com/TheatrClwyd

DEXTER AND WINTER'S DETECTIVE AGENCY

Nathan Bryon

Main Characters

DEXTER, *ten, class clown and only child*
WINTER, *ten, a wannabe detective, Dexter's best mate*
ANGELA, *thirty-six, Mum to Dexter, very cool, has made a big
    mistake*
CARRIE, *thirty-eight, Mum to Winter, very geeky, vegan and
    health-conscious*

Supporting Cast

NEWSROUND PRESENTER
KID 1, 2, 3
GRANNY ANNIE
CALLUM CHARITY BUCKET
BOSSMAN
BARLADY
BILL THE BUTCHER
KATHY COSTUME LADY
JEFF / ZEBRA MAN
TICKET INSPECTOR
POLICE OFFICER

*This text went to press before the end of rehearsals and so may
differ slightly from the play as performed.*

Scene One

We see three ROBBERS *enter stage. They are all dressed like unicorns in onesies and their faces are covered by unicorn masks. They are carrying big 'SWAG' bags. The* ROBBERS *are shouting: 'Grab the bag, don't leave anything… come on LET'S GO!'*

Maybe this could be shown in some funky dance or done with lasers, and we see them break into the jewellery shop and taking all the jewels. We can hear police sirens getting closer and closer.

Scene Two – Newsround Report

SFX – Newsround *theme tune.*

NEWSROUND PRESENTER. Hello, everyone, I'm Ricky, your top stories from *Newsround* this evening. A story we have been following, after two weeks of one of the most intense police searches in British history, three of the four Unicorn Jewellery thieves are in custody this morning.

Scene Three – Dreamland / Bedroom

We see DEXTER *is asleep in bed, he is dreaming. We go into his dream.*

DEXTER. Hi I'm Dexter aka D-Dog, aka Dex, aka Captain Stinkhead, I didn't make the last one up! Welcome to my dreamland, you guys ain't normally here? But that's cool, I'm about to do my favourite thing in the whole world… do you guys want to join in? I said, do you guys want to join in? GREAT!

I wonder who would win in a fight, an elephant or WWE superstar John Cena?

We see the elephant go up against John Cena. John Cena loses BIG TIME and really quickly.

I guess that is a tough battle, what about –

Out of the dream world: we see DEXTER *sniffing asleep in bed, we see* DEXTER *getting out of bed sniffing. His eyes suddenly open!*

BACON!!!!!!!!!! I love the smell of bacon, man, it makes me just wanna eat up the air like YAM YAM YAM YAM!

Today the smell is just wafting around the house and I plan to eat all the bacon.

I run downstairs to get a roll with some ketchup and as if my day couldn't get better, guess who I see tucking into a vegan bacon sandwich, ketchup running down her face…

My best friend and one of the best detectives in the whole entire universe. WINTER!!!!!!

WINTER. YO, Captain STINKHEAD!!! WASSSSSSSUPP!!!!

WINTER runs onto stage and we see them do the coolest complex secret handshake. ANGELA, DEXTER*'s mum, watches them do this handshake.*

ANGELA. Wow, you guys have to teach me that.

WINTER. It's kinda complicated.

ANGELA. I'm a fast learner.

DEXTER. Well we're only gunna show you once.

DEXTER *and* WINTER. So it goes like this, then that, then this, then this and that, then this, that, double that, twist, this this, and that, this, ending on a big fat THAT.

WINTER. Got it?

ANGELA. Ermmm? Yeah, obvs, I'm sure I can wing it.

ANGELA *tries the handshake with* DEXTER, *it goes terribly wrong and* ANGELA *gets whacked left, right and centre.* WINTER *finds this hillllarious.*

WINTER. Maybe we can make a special one for you, Ange? It's called the tortoise.

DEXTER *and* WINTER *make up another secret handshake but it is proper slow like you would for an old person.*

ANGELA. Ohhhhhh I see, you two think you are proper proper funny innit!

DEXTER. We don't think, we know we are...

DEXTER *and* WINTER. JOOOOOKES.

ANGELA. So I'm guessing you guys are so busy being JOKESS you probably don't want what I got...

DEXTER. Depends what you got? If you got a chore rota? You can keep that.

ANGELA. Chore rota? Who do you lot think I am? Mary Poppins? Oooooh it's LOADS better than that?

WINTER. Well if it's those jelly beans with bogey flavour, you can keep that as well.

ANGELA. Funny that, bogey flavour is my favourite! YUMMMMM!

DEXTER *and* WINTER *grimace.*

But nope better than that.

DEXTER. Just tell us, Mum.

ANGELA *pulls out three GIANT VIP queue-jumping tickets to Thorpe Park.*

(*To audience*.) My eyes nearly popped out of my big head, Mum just pulled out three VIP queue-jumping tickets to… THORPE PARK!!!

NOOOOOOOOOOOOOOOOOOOOOOO…

WINTER. WAAAAAAAAAAAAAYYYYYYYYY…

DEXTER *and* WINTER….JOSÉÉÉÉÉÉÉÉÉÉÉÉÉÉÉÉÉ…

ANGELA. My name's Angela, not José and YESSS WAYYYYY, LOSERS!! WHO'S UP FOR IT???

DEXTER *and* WINTER *run around* ANGELA *trying to jump up and grab the tickets out of her hand.*

DEXTER *and* WINTER. ME ME ME ME ME ME ME ME ME ME ME!!!

ANGELA. Right, first one to the car gets to choose the radio station and you lot know how much I love me some Heart FM!

DEXTER AND WINTER. We WANT STORMZY!!!

DEXTER *and* WINTER *RUN!* ANGELA *watches them go and smiles. She goes to catch up.*

Scene Four – Thorpe Park

*We see a movement piece – DEXTER, WINTER and ANGELA
in Thorpe Park – we see big lights, loads of shouting on rides –
we hear loud roller coasters, we see them all eating copious
amounts of junk food, slushies, getting brain-freezes, going on
more rides, winning on the arcade machines. It looks like the
funniest most energetic day EVER!! Below some dialogue that
can be interspersed.*

DEXTER. THORPE PARK IS LITTTT!

DEXTER *and* WINTER. We started on SAW!

Then Detonator!

Scream was WILD!

ANGELA. LUNCHTIME!!!

DEXTER *and* WINTER. CRISPS, BURGER, NUGGETS,
SLUSHIES!

WINTER. BRAIN-FREEEZE!!

DEXTER *and* WINTER. CRISPS, BURGER, NUGGETS,
SLUSHIES!

WINTER. BRAIN-FREEZE.

DEXTER *and* WINTER. Then to finish it off TIDAL WAVE!!!

We hear a big SFX of water splashing.

BEST DAY EVER!!!

Scene Five – Car – Day

'Mans Not Hot' by Big Shaq is blaring. ANGELA *is driving and* DEXTER *and* WINTER *are rapping along to the song in the back.*

The radio goes off suddenly.

DEXTER. MUM! We were listening to that. No way you're putting on Heart FM now.

ANGELA. One sec.

WINTER. We know our rights. Ange, Heart FM is against our human rights.

ANGELA *ignores them, staring out front.*

What was your favourite bit of today, Ange?

ANGELA (*low-energy, not listening*). Yeah.

DEXTER. Mum, Winter said what was your favourite bit?

ANGELA. Hold on.

DEXTER. What? Just answer?

WINTER. What's all those blue lights?

DEXTER. Yeah, Mum, why are all those blue lights outside our house?

WINTER. Are they having a street disco? Sick!

DEXTER *and* WINTER *start practising their dance moves in the back.*

ANGELA. Stay in the car…

WINTER. You better not street disco without us? We can see, you know.

DEXTER. Well before you go, Mum, tell us your favourite part of the day?

ANGELA. Ummm I said I don't know…

DEXTER. Alright, grumpy guts.

ANGELA. I'm sorry –

ANGELA *gets out of the car and starts walking to the house.*

WINTER. Wait, is that the police?

DEXTER. Why are the police running over to Mum?

WINTER. You reckon you've been burgled and they are trying to break the news to her?

DEXTER. BRUV! They better not of touched my Xbox!

WINTER. What? The police are grabbing Ange.

DEXTER *goes to get out of the car.*

ANGELA. STAY IN THE CAR, DEXTER!

DEXTER. What's going on? I need to go and help her, they have obviously made a mistake.

WINTER. But your mum said –

DEXTER *goes to get out of the car and* WINTER *pulls him back.*

Dex, she said stay in the car.

DEXTER. Get off me. They are dragging her into a police van.

DEXTER *opens the car door.*

MUM! GET OFF MY MUM NOW!!!

ANGELA. STAY IN THE CAR, DEXTER!

DEXTER *closes the door. He sits staring outside, concerned.*

Scene Six – Winter's Bedroom

We see DEXTER *sleeping again.*

DEXTER. Ummm I wonder who would win in a fight, my mum versus the police? What? No? I don't want this match? Stop!

We see a police officer come on and grab ANGELA *and drag her off the stage.* DEXTER *wakes up shouting.*

No, stop, get off her, STOP!

WINTER. D-Dog, it's okay, you're okay, you're at my house.

DEXTER *takes a minute to get his bearings.*

DEXTER. What about Mum? Where is she?

There is a knock on the bedroom door. DEXTER *gets his hopes up.*

Enter CARRIE – WINTER*'s mum – she looks very geeky and nasally. She is carrying sandwiches.* Newsround *is on in the background.*

CARRIE. Morning, Dexter, sweetie pie, how are you, darling? Bacon sandwiches? Winter said you love them?

DEXTER *smiles and takes a bite.*

DEXTER. Umm it tastes a bit different.

CARRIE. It's vegan, most people can't taste the difference.

WINTER. Mum, everyone can taste the difference.

CARRIE. Oh, silly me, Dexter, lil update doodah on ya mummy's situmondo.

DEXTER *looks at* CARRIE *confused.*

She asked if you could have a little stay with us for a while, you know, umm while they sort out the whole kerfuffle.

DEXTER. How long for? Is she okay?

CARRIE. She seemed okay, well as okay as one can be, sweetie. Time-wise, darling, we don't know just yet, but mi casa su casa.

WINTER. We can get proper bacon can't we, Mum?

CARRIE. Erm… well I would prefer if we –

WINTER. Can't we, MUM?

CARRIE. Yeah I suppose, darling, I can just use a different frying pan.

WINTER. Dex, we can just see it as a long sleepover. You can even have the top bunk?

DEXTER. Have they said what she did wrong?

CARRIE. Well, darling, I'm sure they have got it all upside down, but umm, they are saying Mummy has umm done something bad.

The police are saying your mum is part of the jewellery robbery.

WINTER. COOOL!

CARRIE. Winter, it's most definitely not cool! If they prove that she did it she will go away for a long time.

WINTER. MUM!

CARRIE. Sorry! I mean I'm sure they won't prove it.

DEXTER. My mum wouldn't do that.

CARRIE. Spot on, champ. So really we have nothing to worry about.

DEXTER. When can I talk to her?

In the background we can hear Newsround *begin.* DEXTER *hears it.*

SHHH!!!

NEWSROUND REPORTER. Next up, all of the suspected jewellery thieves are in custody this morning. Police have located a third of the stolen jewels and plan to recover the rest. Today the fourth suspect will be in court. We go now to our roving report–

DEXTER. Are they talking about Mum?

CARRIE *nods and turns off the TV.*

Scene Seven – Kids' Birthday Party!

DEXTER *and* WINTER *are stood in the middle of the stage. A spotlight on them both. We get the impression everyone is staring at them.*

DEXTER (*to audience*). I thought my day was going to get better. At first it was awesome, Theo is in my class at school and his birthday was at this sick trampoline park, with cool laser lights and loud music, we were just bouncing… Bouncing, bouncing…

We see DEXTER *and* WINTER *bouncing all over the place.*

But the second Carrie left, that's when it started…

KID 1. Oi, Dexter, everyone is saying you know where the jewels are? Do you?

DEXTER. No.

KID 1. Did you help your mum rob it?

DEXTER. No.

KID 2. Someone said that you're rich now? Did you get me an expensive birthday present?

DEXTER. I dunno.

KID 3. Dunno what? Did you know your mum was going to rob the jeweller's?

WINTER. There is no proof she did it, you IDIOT!

KID 1. People are saying your mum did it because she is poor and works at the dump.

DEXTER. My mum's not poor, she just took us to Thorpe Park.

KID 2. Probably her life savings.

Everyone laughs.

DEXTER. MY MUM DIDN'T DO IT!

KID 2. How do we know you're not lying?

I told my mum to not invite you today, in case you robbed my birthday presents.

DEXTER. What?

KID 2. Yeah my dad's been guarding them the whole day, just in case.

DEXTER. Say it to my face.

WINTER. Come on, Dexter, let's go.

DEXTER. NO SAY IT TO MY FACE IF YOU'RE BAD?

KID 2. I DIDN'T WANT TO INVITE YOU TO MY BIRTHDAY IN CASE YOU ROBBED ALL MY PRESENTS! LIKE MOTHER LIKE SON!

We hear a punch SFX. Loads of shouting!

DEXTER (*to audience*). I know, I know, I know, I really shouldn't of done that. I lost it. Theo's nose started bleeding. Carrie got called to pick us up, in the car she was telling me…

CARRIE. Dexter sweetie, darling, I know that you are going through a very hard time, but… you just cannot hit people… it's totally not allowed.

WINTER. But he deserved it, Mum, to be fair he deserved a lot worse.

CARRIE. I don't care, Winter. No one deserves a bust nose on their birthday…

WINTER. He was being SO HORRIBLE to Dexter.

CARRIE. If someone is saying horrible things what are you meant to do…

DEXTER (*to audience*). Carrie was totally right, I'm an idiot! I shouldn't of lashed out!

CARRIE. Dexter, I know I'm not your mummy and I'm not trying to be, promise, but I think you should write a letter of apology!

WINTER. NO WAY!

CARRIE. Madam, stop showing off in front of your friend.

WINTER. I'm not! You weren't even there. I hate you sometimes.

DEXTER. It's fine, Winter, chill. I will write the letter. I'm sorry, Carrie.

Scene Eight – Winter's Room

WINTER *is pacing holding a piece of paper.* DEXTER *is sat down writing his letter.*

WINTER. Can we just send my letter, I think it's proper good. 'Dear Theo, you poo-eating, stinky-breathed, bogey-muncher. It's your own fault you got punched, you shouldn't go round being mean, take this as a life lesson. PS we didn't even want to come to your dumb birthday party, my mum made us go. Yours sincerely, Winter.'

DEXTER. I love that letter bu–

WINTER. Great let me find an envelope…

DEXTER. BUT something tells me that may get us grounded for the rest of our lives. I think I've got it.

WINTER. Go on then, Shakespeare.

DEXTER. 'Dear Theo, I'm so sorry I punched you on your birthday, I feel super bad. I promise I will never punch you again, I got upset about what you were all saying about my mum, you have to understand she is all I have. But that doesn't make what I done okay and I am really sorry, I hope you forgive me.'

WINTER. I guess that's a tiny bit better.

DEXTER *looks sad*.

Dex, you okay?

DEXTER. I mean I've been better, I just KNOW my mum didn't do it.

WINTER. Dude, me too, Ange ain't no teef! We just need other people to believe that.

DEXTER. Yeah… but who is going to believe us, we are just 'kids'.

WINTER. Talk for yourself, I'm nearly eleven. We just need to prove it to everyone.

DEXTER. Yeah but we ain't the Feds.

WINTER. True, but maybe we gather evidence and show the police they are wrong.

We have a light-bulb moment SFX.

DEXTER. I wouldn't even know where to start.

WINTER. Yeah, but whose bestie found the lost hamster in Year 6?

DEXTER. You.

WINTER. Whose bestie found out who was taking the lunch money from the register?

DEXTER. You

WINTER. AND, whose bestie worked out who cheated to win the Connect 4 competition?

DEXTER. YOU!

WINTER. Exactly.

DEXTER *thinks, maybe his belly grumbles.*

DEXTER. Are you thinking what I'm thinking?

WINTER. I really hope so. Let's say it together on three – one, two, three!

DEXTER (*simultaneous*). Let's get fish and chips for dinner.

WINTER (*simultaneous*). LET'S BECOME DETECTIVES!

What?

DEXTER. Sorry, all this thinking got me hungry. YES LET'S BECOME…

WINTER (*simultaneous*). Detectives!

DEXTER (*simultaneous*). Detectives!

WINTER *and* DEXTER *both make detective poses!*

WINTER. So who knows your mum better than anyone else in the world?

DEXTER. Erm… probs Granny Annie?

WINTER. Then we should go and see her to start this INVESTIGATION, BABY!!!!

Scene Nine – St Anne's Care Home

We see GRANNY ANNIE (*eighty-five*) *run on stage in workout gear. 'House Every Weekend' by David Zowie is playing. (I would love* GRANNY ANNIE *to come on stage and get the audience up doing some mini-exercises.)* DEXTER *and* WINTER *are on either side of* GRANNY ANNIE *trying to keep up.*

GRANNY ANNIE. One, two, three, squat. One, two, three, squat. Now star jumps five, four, three, two, one. Now just jumps on the spot, five, four, three, two, one. Now wave your arms up in the air like you just don't care. Come on, no giving up!!!

The music goes down a bit.

DEXTER. Granny, can we chat?

GRANNY ANNIE. Turn it down, Rachel. Course, Dex, on one condition?

DEXTER. What?

GRANNY ANNIE. That you can keep up. SKIPPING!

GRANNY ANNIE *gives* DEXTER *and* WINTER *skipping ropes.* DEXTER *and* WINTER *give each other a look of dread. They all start skipping in time.*

DEXTER. You heard about Mum?

GRANNY ANNIE. What about Angela?

WINTER. Well she got arrested, Annie, for a jewellery robbery.

GRANNY ANNIE. Oh maybe I did read it in the paper.

DEXTER. You don't think she would ever do anything like that do you?

GRANNY ANNIE. Ummm well maybe in her younger years.

WINTER. Huh?

GRANNY ANNIE. Oooh she was a firecracker, but she changed her ways after she was sent to youth detention.

DEXTER. I didn't know about this.

GRANNY ANNIE. HULA HOOPS!!!

> GRANNY ANNIE *drops her skipping ropes and gives*
> DEXTER *and* WINTER *hula hoops to carry on with.*

> Yes, she's not proud of it, love, but she had a rebellious heart
> like me. But after she had you, Dexter, that was it, when she
> learnt she was raising you on her own, she changed her life
> totally around. I've never seen anything like it. She got
> herself a job at the dump and she LOVED IT!

WINTER. What did she do? To you know, get into youth
offenders.

GRANNY ANNIE. I can't quite remember.

DEXTER. Do you think they will let her out, Gran?

> *The dance music stops and* GRANNY ANNIE *stops
> exercising suddenly.*

> I'm just worried, Gran, what if I never see her again?

> *We hear a trumpet SFX indicating lunch.*

GRANNY ANNIE. LUNCHTIME! Gotta go, sweetie. If you
are late to lunch you are stuck with the horrible sandwiches.

WINTER. Eurgh… with crusts on?

GRANNY ANNIE. Ooh I love the crusts, egg mayo urgh! See
you kids later, goood luck!

> GRANNY ANNIE *runs offstage after the sandwiches.*

DEXTER. I didn't even know she got in trouble before.

WINTER. We learnt that your mum is a changed person. That's
what we learnt.

DEXTER. I guess that's good. But what now?

WINTER. Good question, like all my favourite Sherlock books,
we need to get down to the crime scene and start our own
investigation.

DEXTER. They will never let us near the jewellery shop.

WINTER. Of course not, but we can interview witnesses, time to BUILD some of our own evidence. If your mum didn't do it, we need to show all those suckers who did. So tomorrow first stop – the high street!

DEXTER. Tonight, I need a bubble bath, I'm aching, man.

Scene Ten – Local High Street

First up is CALLUM CHARITY BUCKET – CALLUM *is trying to catch people's eyes to talk about his charity.* DEXTER *and* WINTER *are on the high street.*WINTER *is armed with her mobile phone acting as a recording device and a notebook.*

CALLUM. Hi there, could I talk to you for two minutes? No… okay no worries. Hi there, madam, love your hat, can I tell you how you can save a life in just one minute? No, okay no need to burp in my face. Hi –

DEXTER. Hi.

CALLUM *is in shock.*

CALLUM. Wow someone has spoken back to me, that hasn't happened in like three hours.

DEXTER. We were wondering if we can ask you something? Is that okay?

CALLUM. You want to ask about my charity? Wow today is a great da–

DEXTER. Not quite.

WINTER. Where were you on the 17th February around 6 p.m.?

CALLUM. The night of the robbery?

WINTER. So you already know that date. Interesting.

WINTER *writes this down in her notebook.*

CALLUM. Umm sorry, what are you writing down?

WINTER. Stuff?

CALLUM. What stuff?

WINTER. Detective stuff, bruh, relax… unless you got something to hide.

WINTER *writes more down, making* CALLUM *feel on edge.*

CALLUM. Look, I'll talk to you but I need a favour.

Well maybe if you kids help me attract people to the charity.

WINTER. Kids? I'm nearly eleven, mate.

DEXTER. Fine, deal… Can I ask you what you remember?

CALLUM. Oh okay, well on the night of the robbery I was stood on the side of the butcher's, asking people to donate. The odd thing was that the butcher's was closed, shutters down and everything, but it's never usually closed at those times.

WINTER. So all you have to tell us, is the butcher's was closed? What are you hiding?

WINTER *goes closer.*

CALLUM. Erm… nothing… oh yeah I heard three male-sounding voices shouting, it must have been loud, two of the men were in the shop and one was stood outside guarding the place, they were all dressed like unicorns.

WINTER. Good to know, no women's voices?

CALLUM. Nope, then I heard a loud motorbike coming from behind the butcher's, that's when I legged it because I was carrying a bucket of money.

DEXTER. Did you hear or see anything else?

CALLUM. That's it, hope it helped!

DEXTER. Yeah it did. Thanks.

WINTER *and* DEXTER *go to walk off.*

CALLUM. What about our deal?

WINTER *and* DEXTER *turn back, unimpressed. We see* WINTER *and* CALLUM *trying to get money from the public* (*the audience*) *– it's a tough sell.*

Scene Eleven – Newsagent

DEXTER *and* WINTER *enter the newsagent, we hear the door ping!*

BOSSMAN (*to phone*). You said it was a same-day service, I've been waiting for two weeks, don't put me on hold.

DEXTER *and* WINTER. Wagwarn bossman!

BOSSMAN. I've had better days, I've been waiting all day for a person to come round to my shop to fix my CCTV camera after some kids kicked a ball and knocked it out of place. Now it's facing the jeweller's.

DEXTER. Oh no that sucks.

DEXTER *nips outside the shop, we hear the shop door ping.*

BOSSMAN. Yeah it happened two weeks ago.

WINTER. Wait, two weeks? Like the robbery?

DEXTER. The camera is now facing the jeweller's. You gotta have a look.

BOSSMAN. Good idea!

We hear / see BOSSMAN *scrolling through loads of tape with* DEXTER *and* WINTER.

WINTER. You've got footage of the getaway driver… wow, wait, they are not dressed as a unicorn.

DEXTER. The getaway driver is dressed as a zebra?

WINTER. Then everyone jumps on the bike and they ZOOM off.

DEXTER. I haven't heard the police talk about the zebra outfit? All they have mentioned is unicorns.

WINTER. By the time the motorbike came most people ran off apparently.

DEXTER. This is a huge clue, bossman, big up! Come on, Winter, we got a zebra to find.

Scene Twelve – Dexter's Mum's House

WINTER *and* DEXTER *are back at* ANGELA's *flat.*

DEXTER (*to audience*). We just got back to my mum's flat, it's so weird without her here.

Right, I'mma go to my room and get some stuff…

WINTER. Don't forget the Xbox.

DEXTER. That's all I've really come for.

DEXTER *runs offstage.* WINTER *is waiting aimlessly, when there is a knock on the front door. It's a* BAILIFF.

WINTER. Yo.

BAILIFF. Is your mum home?

WINTER. No? Who are you?

BAILIFF. I'm a bailiff, I'm here to collect the money your mum owes us, I've come round here five times already. When is your mum home?

WINTER. I don't live here.

BAILIFF. Then why are you here?

WINTER *goes to close the door. The* BAILIFF *stops it with his foot.*

Tell your mum enough of the games, I haven't got time for this nonsense. She owes us twenty-five thousand pounds and tell her I'll be taking the door off next time I come round.

DEXTER (*off*). Who's at the door, Winter?

WINTER *closes the door.*

WINTER. Oh just a neighbour who is looking for their pet flamingo.

Scene Thirteen – Winter's Bedroom

DEXTER *and* WINTER *are in* WINTER*'s bedroom. They are going over what they learnt today with string and pictures of the people they met.*

DEXTER. So, we met Callum the charity-bucket person, he said the butcher's was closed when it shouldn't be.

DEXTER *and* WINTER *present this evidence using props.*

WINTER. Callum also said he potentially saw the getaway motorbike coming from behind the butcher's, he also said he heard three men's voices, and no women's voices.

DEXTER *and* WINTER *present this evidence using props.*

DEXTER. Then don't forget bossman showed us his CCTV... the getaway driver is a zebra, not a unicorn.

DEXTER *and* WINTER *present this evidence using props.*

WINTER. Not bad for a day's work – tomorrow we go to the butcher's.

Scene Fourteen – Butcher's

There is a butcher – BILL – behind the till. It's an empty shop,
BILL is bored. DEXTER and WINTER walk in. BILL is
excited.

BILL. HII!!!! How are you? Nice to see you? Welcome.

DEXTER. Are you the manager here?

BILL. I wish, I pretend sometimes – (*Silly manager voice.*)
HELLO I'm the manager, you're fired, you're fired. You
want Jeff, he's the big boss, but he's been off for two weeks,
he got a couple more days' leave I think, he's got his kid's
fancy-dress birthday party.

WINTER. Two weeks? That's the same time as the robbery?

BILL. Oh yeah, so it is?

WINTER *writes it down.*

DEXTER. How's business and stuff going?

BILL. Ummm great, business, I mean WOOOO! Never been
better.

WINTER (*coughs*). Lies!

BILL (*his face drops*). Well okay fine, it's been tough. Really
tough.

WINTER. Why?

BILL. Well we are a small business. You have a Tesco at the
end of the road, a Sainsbury's at the other end of the road.

WINTER. I'm sorry to hear that.

BILL. Yeah, but just know Jeff loves this place, he even
remortgaged his house, because he believes everyone should
have the choice to have the best quality meats.

WINTER *writes something down in her notebook.*

WINTER. Well can you tell Jeff to get in touch, we have some
questions we WANT answered!

Scene Fifteen – Street

WINTER. The butcher's is struggling. Interesting.

DEXTER. No, the struggling business is a motive, maybe Jeff did the robbery because his business is running out of money.

WINTER. Yeah maybe, that would make sense. But we need more than that. Loads of people have money worries.

DEXTER. Maybe, but not my mum.

WINTER. Yeah…

It's awkward.

DEXTER. What?

WINTER. Right, next we have to work out where your mum was on the night of the robbery.

DEXTER. WELL, I was having a sleepover at yours. So Mum would of finished work and probably gone to the pub for the quiz.

WINTER. Perfect, let's go check there.

DEXTER. But how we going to get in we ain't eighteen.

WINTER. Where there's a Winter there is a way.

Scene Sixteen – Pub

We see the BARLADY *enter stage, cleaning a glass, she is talking to the audience like they are in her pub.*

BARLADY. Mr Johnson, for the tenth time, wash ya hands when ya come out of the bog.

> I think you have had enough, oi you, get OUT of my pub. Ya barred! I don't care if you're a teacher! Right, you lot know what time it is… KARAOKE time! All the adults stand up! Okay – WE WILL WE WILL ROCK YOU!

The audience join in – they are singing Queen's 'We Will Rock You'.

DEXTER *and* WINTER *creep into the pub,* WINTER *is on* DEXTER*'s shoulders and wrapped in a giant coat and a really funny disguise!*

You're tall!

WINTER *(silly old voice)*. Who me, darling? Yes, I'm a model, didn't you know. I have legs for days, cheekbones for weeks, sweetie.

WINTER starts voguing.

BARLADY. Okay then, what do you want to drink?

WINTER *(silly voice)*. I'll have a Ribena, but in a champagne flute, it's how we all drink it in Paris.

BARLADY. We don't have Ribena.

WINTER *(silly voice)*. No Ribena? Wow, well I never, this clearly isn't The Ritz!

BARLADY. It's a pub,

> Wait a second? How old are you two?

WINTER *(silly voice)*. My playing age? Or my real age? Listen, between you and I… I'm fifty years of age, I've seen a couple world wars, I remember when TVs were black and white, you know.

BARLADY. Really?

WINTER (*silly voice*). Yes, wifi? Just blows my mind.

BARLADY. Disguises off NOW! What do I even pay that bouncer for.

WINTER *jumps off* DEXTER*'s shoulders and they take off their elaborate disguises.*

Dexter, what are you doing here? You're way too young to even think about underage drinking.

DEXTER. I just wanted to know if Mum was in here during the robbery?

BARLADY. I'm sorry to hear about ya mum, she is a right laugh.

WINTER. We just need to prove she was here and that she couldn't of done it.

BARLADY. I'm sor–

DEXTER. No, before you say that, we have already checked at her work, she must of been here, double-check the camera.

BARLADY. Dexter, I'm sorry, but I was working that night.

Mr Johnson started singing 'Let It Be' on the karaoke for two hours straight and I wanted to poke my ears out. Your mum was never here, she would of never let him do that. I'm really sorry.

DEXTER *and* WINTER *look gutted.*

Scene Seventeen – Street

They are just walking down the street.

DEXTER. Sometimes I feel like we are getting somewhere but it's times like that when I think I'm never going to see my mum.

WINTER. Yo, what did I say about positive vibes, D-Dog.

Right listen, so we know the getaway driver is wearing a zebra costume –

DEXTER. So we need to go to the costume shop?

WINTER. Ohhh took the words out of my mouth… let's go!

Scene Eighteen – Costume Shop

DEXTER *and* WINTER *enter the costume shop, they are looking for the person who works in the shop who JUMPS out at them dressed as something funny.*

KATHY. BOO!!!

How can I help you crazy cats? Let me guess you wanna dress up as baby shark? 'Baby Shark… doooo dooo…'

DEXTER. No.

KATHY *doesn't hear the answer and carries on singing.*

KATHY. 'Baby Shark… doo, doo Baby Shark…'

WINTER. No we don't want to dress up as –

KATHY *doesn't hear the answer and carries on singing.*

KATHY. 'BABY SHARK dooo dooo!!'

DEXTER *and* WINTER. WE DON'T WANT TO DRESS UP AS BABY SHARK!!!!

KATHY. No need to shout. How can I help you?

WINTER. Well we are here on some official business.

KATHY. Oooh fancy.

DEXTER. Yeah we just need to find out about your zebra costumes.

KATHY. Well lucky for you, we have one left and let me have a look, ohhh one returning in about one hour.

DEXTER. You have a zebra suit returning in an hour.

KATHY. Yeah but I got one you can take now.

WINTER. How long has that one been out for?

KATHY. I think about two weeks.

WINTER *gives* DEXTER *a look*.

WINTER. Well we will take the zebra suit that is back in an hour.

KATHY. O… kay well I'll see you guys in an hour.

DEXTER. We are gunna wait, this place looks fun.

KATHY. Ohh it is!

Scene Nineteen – Costume Shop – Montage

We see WINTER *and* DEXTER *in the costume shop, trying on various outfits, running around, chasing each other.*

WINTER. Wonder Woman.

DEXTER. Spider-Man.

WINTER. Ninja Turtle.

> *We hear the costume-shop door opening and the music cuts out.*

Scene Twenty – Costume Shop – Later

KATHY *is in the back of the shop, and in comes* JEFF *holding a zebra outfit.* WINTER *and* DEXTER *are staring at* JEFF.

JEFF. Is Kathy around?

DEXTER. She is in the back doing stock.

> WINTER *takes a picture of* JEFF *holding a zebra outfit on her phone.*

JEFF. Okay cool. Did you just take a picture of me?

WINTER. Nope.

JEFF. I think you did.

WINTER. I didn't.

DEXTER. Yeah she didn't. That would be weird.

JEFF. Exactly. Okay well… just tell Kathy I dropped it off please.

WINTER. Sure.

> JEFF *turns around.* WINTER *gets another secret photo,* JEFF *turns around.*

JEFF *looks at them both weird, and leaves the shop. We hear the shop-door SFX.*

DEXTER. Are you thinking what I'm thinking?

WINTER. I hope so, we always get it wrong?

DEXTER (*simultaneous*). LET'S FOLLOW HIM.

WINTER (*simultaneous*). LET'S FOLLOW HIM!

DEXTER. Let's go! See ya later, Kathy.

KATHY. What about the zebra costume…

WINTER. We have changed our mind. BYE GURL!!!!

DEXTER *and* WINTER *run out after* JEFF.

Scene Twenty-One – Street

DEXTER (*to audience*). Winter and I follow zebra man, well he's not dressed as a zebra any more. It's exciting, we are hiding behind cars.

WINTER. DUCK!

DEXTER. Hiding behind trees.

WINTER. Freeze.

DEXTER. Hiding behind bus stops.

WINTER. Roly poly!

DEXTER. Zebra man has his first stop-off, and you will never guess what he does, he only starts looking in jewellery-shop windows.

We hear WINTER*'s camera snap snap snap.*

He must be planning the next shop to rob. This is brilliant.

WINTER. Well for us, not those jewellery shops.

WINTER *takes more snaps on her phone.*

DEXTER (*to audience*). We keep following zebra man but he is starting to act proper Slim Shady, we drop back a bit, we watch more from a distance.

WINTER. Binoculars ready.

WINTER *has made binoculars out of her hands.*

DEXTER. Until suddenly zebra man goes into the train station.

WINTER. He's trying to escape.

DEXTER. Winter and I run after zebra man. Victoria Station is super busy.

We see zebra man about to get on to the train.

WINTER. But we don't have any money for tickets?

DEXTER. Who needs money? (*To audience.*) We…

WINTER. SLIDE.

DEXTER. Under the ticket barriers, We both pick up the *Metro* newspapers and hide behind them and jump onto the train that he gets on.

DEXTER *and* WINTER *lift up their newspapers, which both have eye-holes cut into them.*

WINTER (*to audience*). We have no idea where we're going on the train, all we can see is green fields. Maybe we are going to Scotland?

We hear a phone ping SFX.

My mum is texting saying where are we? Dinner is ready. But I know I can't tell her where we are because we will get in bare trouble!

We watch zebra man go into his pocket, he pulls out this small black box. He opens it and we can't believe what we see!

A big shiny light.

DEXTER. It's a HUGE ring, with a big diamond on it, it looks like something Stormzy would buy his girlfriend. It must be worth LOADS. This must be evidence that it is stolen, he must be on the way to sell it. Suddenly, as our surveillance is going great, we hear…

TICKET INSPECTOR. TICKETS PLEASE! TICKETS PLEASE!

SFX heartbeats.

DEXTER (*to audience*). Winter grabs my arm and says:

WINTER. RUN!

DEXTER. We run into the bathroom. It stinks. I think the ticket inspector may of seen us, DAMN!

Scene Twenty-Two – Toilet

We hear knocking on the door.

TICKET INSPECTOR. Hmm. You know it's a crime to travel without a ticket?

DEXTER (*silly voice*). I'm not a monster, who would ever travel without a ticket?

WINTER *does a massive fart sound.*

Can I have some privacy? My belly is currently erupting.

TICKET INSPECTOR. Umm of course sorry, when you are finished doing what you are doing can you come and find me.

DEXTER (*silly voice*). Of course, good sir!

WINTER *does another massive fart.*

TICKET INSPECTOR. Oh right good okay then… Hope you feel better.

DEXTER (*silly voice*). You may need to put this toilet out of use…

WINTER *does the biggest fart ever heard in the twenty-first century!*

TICKET INSPECTOR. Right… okay. Will inform the crew.

The TICKET INSPECTOR *leaves.* DEXTER *and* WINTER *burst out into laughter. They slowly open the door.*

DEXTER (*to audience*). We looked left and right, no sign of zebra man. Oh no we have lost him. Until –

WINTER. Go, go, go… he's there.

DEXTER (*to audience*). Winter sees zebra man getting off the train at Gatwick Airport. Winter and I run towards the doors, The ticket inspector sees us come out of the bathroom.

TICKET INSPECTOR. OI, you two!

We go into slow motion.

WINTER (*to audience*). The ticket inspector is chasing us as the train doors are closing! Everything goes into slow motion it was like NOOOOOOOOOOOOOOOOOOOOOOOOO OOOOOOOOOOOOOOOOO, we just made it as the doors slammed shut.

DEXTER. We…

WINTER. DUCK.

DEXTER. Behind someone's luggage and follow zebra man, we are waiting in the arrival lounge… It's ages, I wonder who he is waiting for.

WINTER. Then like out of a movie this guy comes through arrivals.

And suddenly zebra man gets on one knee and brings out the BIG expensive ring, the one we saw on the train. The other guy starts crying, he says 'YES'.

DEXTER. Everyone in arrivals is whooping and cheering, even I start clapping until I realise he is our main suspect! Winter takes the final snaps! We have got him exactly where we want him.

DEXTER *and* WINTER. BUSTED!

WINTER. As I'm about to run over to zebra man and do a citizen's arrest!

DEXTER. Two police officers put their hands on our shoulders!

POLICE OFFICER. Got 'EM! We've had reports of two young people who bunked on to the train causing havoc, you both have to come with us!

DEXTER *and* WINTER. Get off us! It's them you need to go and arrest, those two over there, they are thieves!

POLICE OFFICER. Stop causing such a racket! Right let me call your parents!

DEXTER. You can't call my mum she's in jail!

POLICE OFFICER. Typical!

Scene Twenty-Three – Carrie's Car

WINTER, CARRIE *and* DEXTER *are in the car. It's awkward.*

DEXTER (*to audience*). The police called Carrie, I dunno how she got here so fast, we are in trouble!

CARRIE. I am SO disappointed in you both. I've never been called up by the police before.

WINTER. I'm sorry, Mum, but we have cracked it.

CARRIE. Do you know how worried I was? You didn't even text me back?

WINTER. Because I knew you were going to tell us to come home and stop.

CARRIE. Then that's exactly what you should of done.

DEXTER. Carrie, it's my fault, Winter just came along.

CARRIE. Well I appreciate your honesty, Dexter darling, but I am still very disappointed with you as well, I mean what did you even find?

WINTER *and* DEXTER. We have found the getaway driver?!!! It's zebra man!

CARRIE. How? What? When?

DEXTER. Show her the pictures, Winter, we followed this guy who dropped off a zebra suit at the costume shop?

CARRIE. This doesn't sound good...

We hear CARRIE *pull the car over.*

WINTER. One sec... Where is my phone?

We see WINTER *looking for her phone.*

Mum, turn the lights on...

The lights in the car go on...

I don't have it...

DEXTER. What?

WINTER. My phone.

DEXTER. Look again…

WINTER *searches frantically.*

WINTER. I don't.

DEXTER. Where did you leave it?

WINTER. I must of lost it when the police distracted us.

DEXTER. We need to go back now.

CARRIE. I can't, we are two minutes from home. But if you have lost a mobile phone, darling, it will be gone. People pick things up like that.

DEXTER. Why did you lose it?

WINTER. It was an accident, Dex.

DEXTER. Well my mum's never coming out of jail now.

We collected all this evidence and then you just lose the phone? You know how much this meant to me.

WINTER. It was an accident, I'm sorry.

DEXTER. Well detectives don't make mistakes. I just want you to know when my mum is in jail forever, it's all your fault.

WINTER. Well maybe it's your mum's fault.

CARRIE. WINTER!

DEXTER. What?

WINTER *goes into her bag and pulls out some crumpled letters.*

WINTER. When we were at your mum's flat, there was a bailiff at the door, your mum owes them twenty-five thousand pounds.

DEXTER *is devastated.*

CARRIE. Right, enough of this, you two, we are home. Out the car.

DEXTER *and* WINTER *grumpy look at each other.*

NOW!

Scene Twenty-Four – Crime Lab

DEXTER *and* WINTER *sit as far away from each other as possible, both of them sulking.* CARRIE *is in the middle of the lab.* CARRIE *has been looking over all the evidence.*

CARRIE. Right enough of giving each other the silent treatment. Whilst I enjoy the quiet, it's eerie. You're friends, in fact best friends, and Dexter sweetie, darling, mistakes happen, even I make them, if I had a pound for every time I lost my phone I probably would have like five-fifty.

WINTER. Right…

CARRIE. You need two need to make up!

DEXTER *and* WINTER *look at each other. It looks like no one is going to budge until…*

WINTER. I'm sorry, I didn't mean to lose my phone.

CARRIE. Good, Winter… Now… Dexter…

DEXTER. Why didn't you tell me about the bailiff's letter? Partners aren't meant to keep secrets from each other.

WINTER. I just didn't want you to get down. I get it if you don't want to work with me any more.

There is silence.

DEXTER. Remember the time I left our science project on the bus after we stayed up all night making it.

WINTER. I still ain't forgiven you. That tomato-ketchup-erupting volcano was lit.

DEXTER (*laughs*). We all make mistakes, I know that, I'm sorry, fam.

CARRIE. Now do your special handshake thingy?

DEXTER *and* WINTER *do their special handshake, low-energy.*

NO WAY! Come on better than that.

DEXTER *and* WINTER *do it better with more energy.*

BETTER! So now Tweedledee and Tweedledum are back.

I've been looking over all the evidence you have, and you have done a brilliant job so far. So your biggest clues are…

WINTER. The butcher manager Jeff and zebra man.

CARRIE. Nice…

CARRIE *is looking through the evidence more.*

DEXTER. We've never met the manager of the butcher shop as he was away for two weeks, same time as the robbery.

WINTER. But we know zebra man had the zebra costume which means he must of been the getaway driver and then we saw him propose with the stolen jewels at Gatwick.

DEXTER. Stupid idea… And look totally tell me to shut up.

WINTER. SHUT UP!

DEXTER. What?

WINTER. Sorry it was too easy hahahaha.

DEXTER. What if zebra man is the butcher?

A big SFX cue for genius idea. DEXTER *and* WINTER *light-bulb moment.*

WINTER. SHUT UP!

DEXTER. Yeah I knew it was a stupid idea.

WINTER. No I mean a good shut up, like SHUT UP!

CARRIE. That's genius, Dex darling!

DEXTER. Well… I mean… I try.

WINTER. I think you have cracked it. So tomorrow first stop is
the butcher's. The manager should be back by then and if
zebra man is Jeff the butcher we've done it!

CARRIE. Don't forget you're seeing your mum tomorrow
remember.

DEXTER. This will be the icing on the cake.

Let's bring Mum home!

Scene Twenty-Five – Butcher's

DEXTER *and* WINTER *are outside the butcher-shop window,
they are waiting for the shutters to go up.*

DEXTER. I'm nervous…

WINTER. Me too.

We hear the butcher's shutters going up.

Ohh… it's opening up… Oh here we go!!

The shutters are all the way up. DEXTER *and* WINTER
can't wait to see.

Ohhhhh… It's just the guy we saw before.

DEXTER. Oh no. Well that's rubbish.

WINTER. Wait…

DEXTER *and* WINTER. NO WAY JOSÉÉÉÉÉÉÉÉ!

DEXTER. I was right, that's the zebra man and he is wearing the butcher's outfit!

WINTER *takes a picture of him on her mum's phone.*

WINTER. We got him! Zebra man is the butcher manager! Let's get you to your mum!

Scene Twenty-Six – Jail Visiting Area

DEXTER *is sat just facing his mum.*

ANGELA. Now that is a face I want to see. How is my boy?

DEXTER. MUUUUUUUUUUUUUUUM! It's SO good to see you, I've missed you, man, you look different. You look skinny!

ANGELA. I misssed you! Come here let me grab you.

ANGELA *squeezes* DEXTER.

DEXTER. Mum, I have the best news in the entire world.

ANGELA. Oooh what?

DEXTER. I've proved you innocent.

ANGELA. What? Dexter –

DEXTER. Wait a sec, Winter and I have been on your case, night and day. From the moment they arrested you we KNEW you had nothing to do with this, it's just not who you are. We did some of the greatest detective work ever in the world and we think we have found the man who was the getaway driver.

ANGELA. Who?

DEXTER. We found him, he was returning a zebra outfit. It all makes sense.

ANGELA. Dexter.

DEXTER. Why don't you look happy?

ANGELA. Umm –

DEXTER. They probably will have to let you out now? They can't keep you in here, you're innocent. (*Shouting to everyone in the prison.*) MY MUM'S INNOCENT!

ANGELA *takes a moment,* ANGELA *grabs* DEXTER*'s hands.*

ANGELA. Dexter… I'm shocked. Thank you.

No one has ever believed in me like you have.

Look I have to be honest, and I'm sorry.

A beat.

I was the getaway driver, I stored some of the jewels in our flat. Don't go home after this, you hear me?

DEXTER. Has someone in here made you say this?

DEXTER *is looking around angry.*

I'm confused, Mum. But you said… it wasn't you…

ANGELA. No. I did the crime with the guys from the dump. I rented the zebra suit because the costume shop had run out of unicorn suits. I returned it before they arrested me.

Dexter, sometimes adults make mistakes, big ones, they say things –

DEXTER. You lied? I didn't know you could drive a motorbike?

ANGELA. I learnt when I got out of youth offenders, my bike would always break so I would go to the dump to get spare parts.

DEXTER. Do I even know you?

ANGELA. I wasn't thinking. You telling me you have proved me innocent, has made me realise I can't keep lying any more.

The debt just piled and piled up and I saw a way out, at least I thought it was a way out.

DEXTER. Yeah, a way out of my life.

ANGELA. It's the worst thing I've ever done, I thought money was more important than love.

DEXTER. I didn't need all the presents you bought? I need you.

Mums don't make mistakes.

ANGELA. We do.

Dexter, please, I can make it up to you. I will be out soon, thing will be different.

DEXTER. Don't lie again, please!

ANGELA *goes up to hug* DEXTER, *he pulls back*.

ANGELA. Dexter, please don't leave like this.

DEXTER *gets up to leave*.

Scene Twenty-Seven – TV Report

NEWSROUND REPORT. Here at *Newsround* we have breaking news, the getaway driver in the Unicorn Robbery has plead guilty getting a reduced sentence of five years for providing evidence as to where the last unfound jewels were kept. Police detectives raided a two-bedroom flat and found the most expensive stone stuffed into floorboards in a child's room.

BIG SFX of JAIL DOORS SLAMMING!

Scene Twenty-Eight

DEXTER *is in his dream state.*

DEXTER. I wonder who would win in a fight – my mum versus
a judge.

We see a JUDGE *enter the stage.*

JUDGE. I sentence you to five more years!

ANGELA. No, please!

JUDGE. Order, order!

DEXTER. No, no… she's done her time, she's done her time,
you've got to let her out!

We see ANGELA *banished to prison,* DEXTER *is really
stressed.*

WINTER *enters stage.* DEXTER *is clearly having
a nightmare…*

WINTER. Dex, Dex, it's okay… you're having a nightmare,
today's the day!

WINTER *drags* DEXTER *offstage, excited.*

Scene Twenty-Nine

DEXTER (*to audience*). I've been going to see Mum every
weekend, we even write to each other. We have talked more
now she was in prison than we would when she was home.
Don't get me wrong, it's not been easy. Mum's missed
bare things, but I've forgiven her, totally, I get it. We all
make mistakes, you just have to put your hands up and say,
I was wrong!

Scene Thirty – Outside Prison

WINTER *is leant up against the wall,* DEXTER *is pacing outside the prison.*

DEXTER. Well what if they aren't letting her out? Then what?

WINTER. That won't happen?

DEXTER. It's just we have been waiting ages?

WINTER. Be patient bro, soon.

DEXTER. Well I've waited five years, I guess what's another fifteen minutes.

    DEXTER *carries on pacing.*

    What if? She don't wanna come out? What if she has made friends and prefers it in there.

WINTER. Dex, you spoke to her last night on the phone, she sounded so excited.

    WINTER *stares and smiles at* DEXTER .

DEXTER. Then where is she? Why are you smiling?

WINTER. It's just I ain't seen you this happy in ages. Don't tell ya girlfriend I said that – (*Laughs.*)

DEXTER. Well of course Abby and I are happy but this is different, MUMSY IS FINALLY COMING HOME!!!! Well at least I hope…

WINTER. You think she will enjoy our surprise?

DEXTER. I hope so, man! Oh yeah… thanks innit.

WINTER. For what?

DEXTER. I dunno, for everything, you been there for me the whole time, this would of been impossible without you, I literally couldn't ask for a better friend.

WINTER. You gunna miss living with me innit?

DEXTER. Well not hearing you sing in the shower?

WINTER. Bruv, you wish you had a voice as good as mine…
But don't worry, Dex, you can come and visit.

DEXTER. Yeah I will come beat you on Xbox real quick.

WINTER. Keep dreaming. We don't got time for Xbox anyway,
think we got our next detective case lined up.

DEXTER. Oooh what is it?

WINTER. Well I'll give you a couple days off with ya mum,
but for our next mission we have to get on a plane.

DEXTER. Ooooh that sounds SICK!

We hear the gates open. ANGELA *walks through with
a plastic bag full of stuff over her shoulders.* DEXTER *sees
her, he jumps up and then tries to play it cool.* ANGELA
runs over to DEXTER *and gives him a big hug almost
picking him up.*

ANGELA. 'SUP, SUCKERS!!!

DEXTER. Rare, Mum, you got them hulk muscles? Picking me
up like that.

ANGELA. What is my boy too big for a squeeze? I've wanted
to do that for ages.

DEXTER *hugs* ANGELA *back.*

DEXTER. I'm so GASSED to see you.

ANGELA. So what to see me ?

DEXTER. Gassed? It's slang?

WINTER. It means happy.

ANGELA. Wow now my son speaks another language, I've got
a lot to catch up on – (*Laughs.*)

ANGELA *hugs* WINTER.

WINTER. 'Sup, Ange! Great to see you!

ANGELA. Lovely to see ya, thanks for looking after him.

We hear a car horn beep! SFX we hear CARRIE *shout out:*
'COME ON, SLOW COACHES!!!'

DEXTER. Ohh yeah we better bounce?

ANGELA. What?

WINTER. It means we should get going.

ANGELA. Why?

DEXTER. Well we are going to… (*Drum roll.*)

WINTER (*simultaneous*). Thorpe Park!

DEXTER (*simultaneous*). Thorpe Park!

And this time we getting all the way home!

ANGELA. First one to the car gets to pick the radio station!
Bring on Heart FM!

ANGELA *runs ahead!*

DEXTER *and* WINTER. We STILL want Stormzyyyy.

Stormzy's 'Vossi Bop' plays us out –

The End.

A Nick Hern Book

Dexter and Winter's Detective Agency first published in Great Britain as a paperback original in 2019 by Nick Hern Books Limited, The Glasshouse, 49a Goldhawk Road, London W12 8QP, in association with Paines Plough and Theatr Clwyd

Dexter and Winter's Detective Agency copyright © 2019 Nathan Bryon

Nathan Bryon has asserted his right to be identified as the author of this work

Cover illustration by Steffi Holtz

Designed and typeset by Nick Hern Books, London
Printed in the UK by Mimeo Ltd, Huntingdon, Cambridgeshire PE29 6XX

A CIP catalogue record for this book is available from the British Library

ISBN 978 1 84842 890 4

Woodland
CARBON
www.woodlandcarbon.co.uk
NICK HERN BOOKS
Printed on Carbon Captured paper

www.nickhernbooks.co.uk

facebook.com/nickhernbooks

twitter.com/nickhernbooks